Two Years Before the Mast

by Richard Henry Dana

Abridged and adapted by JOHN M. HURDY

Illustrated by DENNIS DIERKS

A PACEMAKER CLASSIC

Fearon Education
a division of
Pitman Learning, Inc.
Belmont, California

PACEMAKER CLASSICS

Robinson Crusoe
The Moonstone
The Jungle Book
The Last of the Mohicans
Treasure Island
Two Years Before the Mast
20,000 Leagues Under the Sea
Tale of Two Cities

ISBN 0-8224-9235-X

Printed in the United States of America.

Contents

1 How I Became a Sailor

Boston harbor was filled with ships. Some of them had just come back from Europe, India, and even China. Other ships were about to sail. The *Pilgrim* was one of them. She was getting ready for the long trip around South America to California.

It was August 14, 1834. This was the day the *Pilgrim* would sail. She would not get back to Boston harbor for two years. And I—Richard Henry Dana —would be on her! I still found it hard to believe.

I had been going to school at Harvard College. Then my eyes started to go bad. I went to the doctor, but he could not help. "There is nothing I can do," the doctor said. "Your eyes need a rest. You must get away from your books for a while. A year or two at sea might help." So I left Harvard and signed on the *Pilgrim*. I was going to be a sailor.

Dressed in my new sailor clothes, I boarded the *Pilgrim*, ready to go. I wanted very much to look like a sailor. But I knew that I did not. A real sailor—a "salt"—has a way of wearing his clothes. And when he moves, he has a rolling walk. Never having been to sea before, I was just a "green hand," as sailors say. And anyone who looked at me could tell. Sailor clothes alone can not turn a man into a sailor. There is only one way a green hand can turn into a salt—by sailing.

Late in the afternoon, the time came to set sail. I knew nothing about working on a ship. I just did what I was told, and tried to do it right. Soon, everything was ready. The *Pilgrim* began to move out of the harbor. I could feel the waves splashing on the front of the ship. We were under way!

Up to this time, we had not seen our captain. But now that we were at sea, he came up on deck. He walked up and down, saying nothing, just looking at us. If Captain Thompson liked what he saw, he did not show it. At last, he turned and stopped.

"Men," the captain said, "we are starting on a long trip. If we get along well together, it will be a good trip. If you do just as I say, we can be friends. But if you don't, you will wish you had never signed on the *Pilgrim*. That is all I have to tell you. Now get back to work!"

And back to work we went.

I soon learned that I was not the only green hand on board. Working next to me was a sailor named Stimson.

"Is this your first time at sea?" he asked.

"Yes," I answered. "It is not hard to spot a green hand, is it?"

"Well, you are not alone," Stimson said. " I am a green hand, too."

We both laughed. "Where are you from?" I asked.

"Boston. And where are you from?"

"I am from Boston, too!"

We found that we knew many of the same people in Boston. We talked until the sun set. Then Stimson had to take his turn as look-out. I was left alone.

I liked Stimson, but being alone pleased me, too. Everything was so quiet. The ship moved along over the dark sea almost without a sound. In the black sky, bright stars were shining all around. It was a beautiful night. I thought about my home in Boston and my friends at Harvard. I also thought about the next two years at sea. What would happen in that time? What new places and things would I see?

In no time at all, I heard seven bells ring. That was the sign that my watch was over. Now I could go below and get some rest.

Sailors live and sleep below the deck in the front part of the ship. The captain has the back part of the ship to himself. No one else may go there. The sailors must stay up front—"before the mast," as they say.

The place where I was to live was small and dark. It was filled with rope, sails, and the ship's stores. With six other sailors on board, there was little room for any of us. I had no bed. And I had no place to put my clothes. And to top it off, I was beginning to get sick.

I was not used to the rolling of the ship. I lay down on some sails and tried to sleep. But every time I closed my eyes, I felt sick. The ship began to roll even more. I could hear the wind blowing. Then I heard the sound of rain falling. A storm was coming up.

I could hear men moving about. Then I heard a loud cry. "All hands on deck!" the mate called. "Get up here and take in sail!"

When I got on deck, I could see that the storm was a bad one. The ship was almost over on her side because of the strong wind. Each time she rolled, great waves would break across the deck. Water was splashing over everything, wetting us to the skin.

Ropes and sails were blowing about like things gone wild. I had a hard time just keeping on my feet. I still did not have my "sea legs." And the rolling of the ship made me sick again. But no one had time to care about me. There was work to be done.

"Get aloft, Dana!" said the mate. "Get up the rigging and help the others take in sail."

This was the first time I had ever been sent aloft. I had to climb up the rigging to the top of the mast. How I got there, I will never know. I was not much help to the other men up there with me. The deck was so far below it looked like part of a toy ship. I held on to the rigging with all my might, more sick than ever.

At last we were done and were told to go below deck. As bad as it was on deck, I was in no hurry to go below. My new home was no better than a dark, wet hole. No sailor ever had such a bad time, I thought.

And this was just the first day out. I did not think that I could stand it for two years. I wanted to go home.

For three days the storm went on. Then one morning it began to let up. My watch that day was before breakfast. The first thing we did on the morning watch was wash the deck. It was hard work. By the time we were finished, I was tired and hungry. I sat down to wait for seven bells, the call to breakfast.

The mate walked over to me. "What do you think you are doing?" he said.

"I am all done with my work," I answered. " So I am waiting for breakfast."

"A sailor is *never* finished with his work," said the mate. "No one sits and rests when he is on watch. Get aloft. The top mast needs painting."

I still felt a little sick. But, sick or not, a sailor must do what he is told. I climbed up the rigging with a can of paint. On deck, the rolling of the ship was not so hard to take. But high on the mast, it was too much for me. I got sick again.

Then, at last, I heard seven bells. I finished painting and climbed down to the deck for breakfast. The ship's cook was a kind man. He knew how sick I had been. "My boy," said the cook, "the storm is about over. Now you are ready for a sailor's breakfast. Eat this good salt meat and ship's bread. It will make a new man of you. Eat it all. Then you will be on your way to being a sailor."

6

2 On Board the *Pilgrim*

For the next few days, the sky was bright and blue. With a good wind behind her, the *Pilgrim* sailed on, mile after mile. As time went by, I began to learn how a ship is run.

The captain is the head of the ship. He gives the orders. The officers and sailors carry them out. The captain stands no watch and does as he pleases. No one can tell him what to do. He can be on deck as much or as little as he wants. On the other hand, he is alone most of the time. The captain has no friends on board. He must keep to himself.

The officers stand between the captain and the sailors. The first mate is the head officer. The captain tells the mate what he wishes to be done. Then the mate gives the orders to the sailors and the other officers. The mate keeps a close eye on everything. He sees to it that every man does his work. The other officers also make sure that the sailors are kept busy.

On board ship, the kitchen is called a "galley." The captain may not have any friends on board. But every sailor wants to be the cook's friend. The cook always has a fire going in his galley. On cold nights, he sometimes lets the men come in to get warm. He also lets the sailors dry their wet clothes by the fire.

A ship can not sail by herself. Day or night, some sailors have to be on watch. While some of the men sleep, others are on watch. One watch begins in the morning and ends in the afternoon. Another watch takes over for the night. In between, there is the "dog watch." This is a short watch that lasts from four in the afternoon to seven at night. It is the only time when everyone is on deck together.

Not every man has to work during the dog watch. It is the only time of day when there is not much to do. The captain stands, looking out to sea. The officers walk up and down the deck together. In his galley, the cook sits down for a quiet smoke. The sailors sit around, telling stories or singing songs. Then the sun sets and the dog watch ends. Some of the men go below to sleep, while others begin the next watch.

There may not be much work on the dog watch. But there is a lot to do all the rest of the day. As soon as the sun was up, we had to be on deck working. We started even before we had breakfast. At first, I thought that we were just getting the ship ready for the trip. "Soon," I said, "the hard work will be over. Then there will be nothing to do but sail the ship."

But this did not happen. We kept working hard, day in and day out. There was always something to do. Everything on a ship wears out fast. It is the sailors' work to keep fixing her up. We were busy painting, washing, and fixing things all day long.

When there was nothing else to do, we made rope. The sun, the sea, and the wind wear out rope in a few weeks. And there is nothing a ship needs more than rope. There are miles of rope on a ship. The sails are pulled up and down with rope. The masts are kept in place with rope. And everything below deck is tied down with rope.

The sailors do most of the heavy work. But the officers also have things to do. One of the officers on board did not do his work well. On top of this, he often fell asleep on watch. Mr. Foster, the officer, came from a good family. His father had sent him to the best schools. But Mr. Foster did not work at school. And now, he was not working at sea.

When he should have been working, he stood around talking and joking. He did not keep himself busy. And he did not care if the sailors kept busy. You may be surprised to find that we did not like this. Sailors want their officers to be kind. But they like the officers to keep them on their toes.

One night, Mr. Foster and I were on watch together. He was the officer of the watch. Rain had been falling on and off, and now the wind was springing up. "We may be in for another storm, Mr. Foster," said the captain. "Stay ready." The captain turned and went below.

"You heard what the captain said," Mr. Foster told the sailors. "Keep a close watch." Mr. Foster walked up and down the deck a few times. But after a while, he became tired. He lay down on the deck and was soon asleep.

Not long after, Captain Thompson came back. He saw Mr. Foster sleeping, but he did not say anything. Just then, Mr. Foster woke up and saw the captain. He did not want Captain Thompson to know he had been sleeping. So he made believe he had just closed his eyes for a minute. He began sing-

ing to himself. Then, without looking at the captain, he stood up. He walked over to a sailor and gave him an order.

But Mr. Foster's plan did not work. "You can not trick me!" Captain Thompson roared. "I saw you sleeping. You good-for-nothing! You are not a man, a boy, or a sailor! You are no better than a *thing* on board this ship. Go below! I'll stand the rest of your watch."

The next morning, the captain called all hands on deck. He made Mr. Foster stand up before us. "This man," the captain said, "is not fit to be an officer on this ship. He is not fit to be an officer on *any* ship. From now on, he will be a sailor like the rest of you. He will take orders like a sailor. And he will do a sailor's work. After today I don't want to hear anyone calling him *Mr.* Foster. Foster is good enough for him."

The captain left Foster where he was and walked over to us. "I'll need a man to take Foster's place," he said. Then he turned to the sailor standing next to me. "Jim Hall, you are the best sailor on this ship. From now on, you are an officer."

The captain looked at the rest of us. "This man is the new officer. You will call him *Mr.* Hall. And you will follow Mr. Hall's orders just as you follow my orders."

3 Cape Horn

Day after day the *Pilgrim* sailed on. Weeks went by. Summer left us and fall came. By the time we neared Cape Horn, it was almost winter. Here, on the far end of South America, there are storms almost every day. Waves as high as the top of a ship's mast have been seen. And the wind is as cold as ice.

Many a ship has gone down trying to sail around Cape Horn. And many a sailor has been killed. Not a man on board the *Pilgrim* wanted to sail around the Cape. But there was no other way to get to California by sea.

Another day went by. The next morning, there was still no sign of the Cape. The wind was light and the sun was shining. "A few more miles and we should spot the Cape," said Mr. Hall. "Keep watch for land." But all we could see was water and sky.

Early in the afternoon, the wind became strong. It was blowing from off the Cape, and blowing hard. When my watch was done, I went below for dinner. I could feel the ship rocking as I ate. No one felt much like talking. We sat and waited, listening to the wind. Then, just as the sun was setting, came the cry, "All hands on deck!"

We threw down our dishes and hurried up on deck. The ship was sailing straight into a black cloud. The cloud rolled along, covering the sun. Everything turned dark. "Here comes Cape Horn!" said Mr. Hall.

In a few minutes the storm was upon us. Never have I seen such a heavy sea. The waves seemed to be a mile high. They rolled over our ship from all sides, covering the deck with water.

"Get aloft and take in sail!" cried the mate. Up we went. The wind roared in our ears. And the hard rain bit into our faces. But there was no time to think about the storm. We had work to do. If we did not get the sails in, the wind would break the mast.

This was the end of warm days and quiet seas. In the days before us, we would meet storm after storm. Until we got around Cape Horn, we would have no rest.

By the next morning, the storm had let up. But it was very cold. When I went on watch, I found the deck covered with snow. We pulled up our sails again, and went on. But as night came, the storm was back again.

On night watch, it was my turn to steer the ship. This was my "trick at the wheel," as sailors call it. I had never steered in such a heavy sea before. I tried hard to do everything right.

It takes time to learn how to steer a ship right. The ship must head into the waves just so. With the wind blowing as strong as it was, this was hard to do. I had to be careful. If I was not, the waves might wash everything off the deck. Though I was still a green hand, I steered well enough to please the officer. I was pleased, too.

The next few days were not so bad. But then we had a real storm come at us. Large gray clouds filled the sky. They rolled across the sea right at us. We knew we were in for a bad storm.

"Get aloft, men!" said the mate. "Take down all sails." We worked as fast as we could. But there was not enough time. The storm hit us before we were finished.

The sky turned black. From the rigging where we were, we could not even see the deck below. Heavy snow began to fall. Soon the ropes and rigging were covered with it. Our hands were so cold we almost could not move them. But we kept working. The sails became coated with ice. We had a hard time taking them down.

At last, we were finished. We climbed down to the deck as fast as we could. There was nothing more to do for now but hold on. The waves came roaring down on the ship. Each wave seemed bigger than the one before. One minute, the ship would be high in the air on top of a wave. The next minute, we would be up to our necks in water.

For three days the storm went on. All of our clothes were wet. We had nothing dry to put on. As soon as we finished our watch, we would take our wet clothes off to dry. Then we would lay down to sleep until our watch was called again.

A sailor can sleep at any time in any place. No sound of wind or water can wake him. He is too tired to care. We were always fast asleep when our watch was called in the morning. When we woke, we found that our clothes were still wet. There was nothing to do but put them back on.

Because of the storm, even getting our food was hard work. We ate below, but got our food from the galley on deck. When we were out of meat, one of us went to the cook. He gave the sailor a side of salt meat. A side of meat is as big as a man.

Carrying a thing like that took some doing. Even when the sea was quiet, it was hard work. In a storm, with the ship rolling, the man had to be very careful. Often, as the sailor carried the meat, a large wave would hit the ship. Knocked down by the water, the man would go rolling across the deck. Many a time both man and meat were almost washed over the side.

Captain Thompson would not let us eat in the galley. He would not even let us drink our hot tea there. We had to go below to drink it. The tea was often cold before we could get below.

One sailor tried running from the galley carrying his tea. Just then, a high wave hit the ship. Water raced across the deck, knocking the man off his feet.

For a minute, we could not even see him. When he got back up, he was still holding his cup. But his tea was gone. All that was in the cup now was cold water. The sailor laughed. "A man is no sailor if he can not take a joke," he said.

It was a hard joke. We needed our hot tea to help keep us warm. One large cup a day was all anyone got. That gone, no matter how, there was no more for the day. But the rest of us would not let the poor man go without. We each gave him a little of our own tea.

The day after this happened, we said good-by to Cape Horn. After a week of hard sailing, we were now west of the Cape. Every man on board was glad to see the last of it.

4 The Sea Takes a Man

What a black day it was! We lost a man to the sea. I was below, fast asleep, when the cry came: "All hands on deck! Man in the sea!"

We jumped up and hurried on deck. The officer of the watch had stopped the ship. No one was even steering her. The sailor who had been at the wheel had run over to the side. He was trying to throw a rope to the man in the sea.

The other sailors were just putting a boat into the water. I ran over in time to jump in with the others. Next to me in the boat was my friend Stimson. I asked him who was in the sea. "George Ballmer," he said.

George was from England. He was as nice a man and as good a sailor as you will find. We all liked him. I wondered if we could save him.

"How did it happen?" I asked.

"George was going aloft when he fell," Stimson told me. "He must have lost his hold."

We looked for George for a long time. But there was no sign of him. He did not know how to swim. And he was wearing heavy clothes when he fell. He must have gone down at once.

After a while, we knew there was no point in looking any more. Even so, we kept on looking. We did
not want to give up. No one wanted to go back to the
ship. But, at last, the time came when we had to go
back.

As soon as we got back to the ship, Captain Thompson sent for us. "Is there any use in taking more time to look for George?" he asked.

"No, Captain," one of the sailors answered. "He is gone. . . . He is at the bottom of the sea."

"Then," Captain Thompson said, "we must get on our way. Staying here will not bring George back."

No one said a word as we pulled the sails up. The wind filled them, and in a minute we were moving again.

When a sailor is killed at sea, his captain must sell his things right away. That is so the man's things will not get lost. And by selling them, the captain gets some money to give to the poor man's family. Captain Thompson had George's trunk brought up. In a short time, everything was sold off. By the next watch, there was nothing left on board that belonged to George.

It was as though George Ballmer had never been on the *Pilgrim*. When the sea takes a man, it takes everything. The man is gone, never to be seen again. Nothing is left, nothing at all.

But it is hard to believe that the man is not still on the ship. You keep thinking that you will see him again. And you miss him all the time. There are so few sailors living on a ship. When one is gone, he leaves a hole that can not be filled. It was as though we had lost an arm. Everything we did seemed to make us think of him. But he was gone.

The next morning, we spotted the island of Juan Fernandez. At first, it looked like a little blue cloud coming out of the sea. But soon we saw that it was an island. We could see hills and trees, and a few houses.

By afternoon, we were sailing into the harbor. We pulled down the sails and let the anchor run out. It was the first time we had anchored since leaving Boston, 103 days before.

I was pleased to be near land again. On watch that night, I could smell flowers. And I could hear frogs. It was almost like being home.

The *Pilgrim* had stopped at Juan Fernandez for fresh water. In the morning, Mr. Hall picked five men to go with him to the island. I was one of the men he picked. We got the boat ready and rowed away from the ship.

While men from the island were getting the water, we had time to walk around. Along the street women were selling fruit. It looked good, so we got some. We had not had any fruit for a long time. I also had a cup of milk. On board ship, there was only water and tea to drink.

Our visit was much too short for me. I could have stayed on the island for days. But it was time to row back to the ship. We put the fresh water on board and got ready to go. The men on watch pulled up the anchor, and we were soon under way. By the time night came, we had left Juan Fernandez far behind us.

A few days after we left the island, Stimson and I had good news. We had been after the captain to let us bunk with the other sailors. The rest of the sailors bunked in the forecastle. But we were green hands. And green hands are always put near where the officers sleep. That way, the officers can keep an eye on them. Stimson and I felt we had learned enough to be on our own. Captain Thompson must have thought so too, because he let us make the move.

As soon as we were in the forecastle, we began to feel like real sailors. We had our own bunks. We had places to keep our clothes. We could do as we pleased. When we were close to the officers, we had been afraid to make any noise. And the other sailors had looked down on us. To them, we were just green hands, just puppies.

Now, Stimson and I felt we were as good as anyone. And the others thought so too. We laughed, played, and smoked together. No man can call himself a sailor until he has lived in the forecastle. He must get up and go to bed with the other sailors. He must eat from their dishes and drink from their cups. He must listen to their stories and learn their ways. After I had been there a week, I knew my days as a green hand were over. Now I, too, was a sailor.

5 California

With a good wind filling our sails, the *Pilgrim* moved on. South America was behind us now, and soon we would be in California. Six weeks went by. Then we turned east. Soon, we were near land again. Because of this, we stopped sailing at night. Captain Thompson did not want to run his ship into the rocks.

Our first stop was Santa Barbara. We got there January 14, after 150 days at sea. In California, a strong wind blows off the sea from November to April. When a storm comes up, the wind can drive a ship into the rocks. And Santa Barbara has nothing that can be called a harbor. Because of this, we had to stay well away from the land. We anchored three miles out.

Not far from us, another ship was anchored. "What ship is that?" I asked. One of the sailors knew about her. "That is the *Ayacucho*. She carries goods between California and the Sandwich Islands."

"She is a fine looking ship," I said.

"And she is fast, too," the sailor answered. "She can make the *Pilgrim* look like a turtle."

Across the water, I could see the mission and town of Santa Barbara. Many of the buildings were painted white. A little behind them stood the mission, also painted white. Behind both was a ring of hills. Grass was growing on the hills, but there were no trees. I was told that some years back a great fire had killed all the trees. But, trees or not, Santa Barbara was a beautiful place.

That afternoon, Captain Thompson went into town. He told us to pick him up at the end of the day. We put the boat into the water just as the sun was setting. A strong night wind was beginning to blow. As we neared the beach, we could hear heavy waves breaking on the sand. We stopped before we were too close.

"How do we get by this?" I asked.

"I don't know," said Stimson. "Those waves could break our boat in two."

"Wait a minute," said another sailor. "Here comes a boat from the *Ayacucho*. Most of the sailors on that ship are from the Sandwich Islands. You know what good sailors Sandwich Islanders are. Let's see how they do it."

The men from the *Ayacucho* rowed their boat right up to the breaking waves. Then they stopped and waited. Behind them a great wave was starting to roll in. As it got near, they began to row. The wave caught up with them and carried them along with it. The boat raced along the top of the wave like a sled on a hill. As the wave began breaking on the beach, the men jumped out. In a minute, they had pulled their boat up high and dry on the sand.

We saw at once what we must do. The trick was to keep the back end of the boat facing the waves. We could not let any waves hit the side of the boat. If a wave hit us on the side, we would turn over.

We turned the boat until it was facing the right way. Then we waited for a wave. As the wave rolled in behind us, we began rowing with all our might. It was hard work keeping the end of the boat into the wave. But we did it. The boat took off like an arrow. We were on the beach before we knew it.

The men from the *Ayacucho* were busy working. They were filling their boats with hides. This was to be the *Ayacucho's* cargo—dry hides of cows. As we waited for Captain Thompson, we stood and watched. The *Pilgrim's* cargo would also be hides.

Two of the sailors from the *Ayacucho* had pulled their boat back into the water. They had a hard time holding it in place. Again and again they were almost knocked off their feet by the waves. Other sailors were bringing the hides to the boat. The hides were long and heavy. They were as hard as boards. To keep them out of the water, the sailors carried them on their heads.

One of our sailors turned to me. "Well, Dana," he said, "do you think you will like this kind of work? It is not much like your work at Harvard, is it? But it is still 'head work!'" He laughed at his joke. I laughed, too. But I did not think I was going to like this 'head work.'

Back on the ship that night, we had fresh meat for dinner. "Eat all you want, men," we were told. "As long as we are in California, we will have fresh meat." After eating salt meat for so many weeks, that was good news.

That night we left for Monterey. Captain Thompson had brought a friend of his back with him. The man lived in Santa Barbara, but was going with us to Monterey.

By morning, a strong wind was blowing. All the sails on the *Pilgrim* were up. We raced along. I had never seen the ship move so fast before. By afternoon, there was even more wind. The ship seemed almost to be flying.

"What is the captain doing?" asked one of the

sailors. "In this wind, we should take down some sail. If we don't, something is going to break."

"The captain is showing off," another man said. "He wants his friend to see how fast the *Pilgrim* can go."

The wind blew even more. A storm was coming up. We waited for the captain to tell us to take in sail. But he said nothing. All at once, there was a loud pop, then another. The ropes were breaking. It would not take long for the wind to cut the sails to pieces.

Springing aloft, I climbed for the top sail. Sails and ropes banged into me as I climbed. The top sail was swinging from side to side. I could not catch hold of it.

On the deck, the sailor at the wheel saw what was happening. He told another sailor to help me. The man caught hold of the top sail's ropes and pulled down on them. This kept the top sail from swinging so much. In a few minutes, I had the sail tied down.

We all had our hands full. Every man was busy. I could see Stimson across from me on the other mast. He was trying to tie down a sail. But the wind kept pulling the sail out of his hands. It took time and hard work, but at last we had everything back in place. This was the last time Captain Thompson tried showing off for a while.

We had five days of rain and wind. Heavy seas made the ship roll. Captain Thompson's friend, who was no sailor, got quite sick. The wind blew us far out to sea. When the storm was over, it took us four days to get back close to land. At last we sailed into Monterey.

The harbor at Monterey has a wide mouth. But it is also very long. At the far end of the harbor, the water is always quiet. No storm could get to us here.

I liked Monterey even better than Santa Barbara. The hills around the town were green with trees. All the houses were painted white and topped with red roofs. Each house had its own little garden. Everything was clean, shining, and pleasing to the eye.

The next day was Sunday. On most Sundays, we sailors did not have to work much. We thought Captain Thompson would let us visit the town. But he did not. The top of one of our masts was wearing out. We were told to put up a new mast.

We were not happy about having to work on our day off. "Captain Thompson knows Sunday is the only time we have to rest," said one man. "This work does not have to be done today. It could wait until tomorrow."

"But what can we do?" another sailor said. "If the captain tells us to work, we have to work."

The mate knew how we felt. "Keep at it, my boys," he said. "When you are finished, you can take the boat and go fishing." This made us feel a little better. But from that day, we liked Captain Thompson even less than before.

6 Head Work

The next morning, we began bringing our cargo up on deck. We had come to Monterey to sell it. After a while, the deck looked like a store. We had brought all kinds of things with us from Boston. There were boxes of nails and cans of paint, tables, chairs, and wagon wheels. We had bowls and dishes, coats, suits, dresses, and hats. We even had toys and candy.

The people of Monterey came out to the *Pilgrim* in small boats. For ten days, the ship was filled with people. Men brought their families to look and to buy. Children were running all over the deck. Women in bright-colored dresses stood around talking in Spanish. Their voices were soft and full of music.

Because California belonged to Mexico then, all the people talked in Spanish. Not many people knew English. We were going to be in California for a long time, so I began learning Spanish. I listened with care to every word I heard. I also got a book of Spanish words. Soon, I knew enough Spanish to talk with the people.

This turned out to be a good thing for me. The other sailors could not speak any Spanish at all. One day Captain Thompson heard me talking in Spanish. From then on, he always sent me to town to get goods for him. Sometimes I did not know the Spanish word for the thing he wanted. But I never told him so. When I got to town, I would go into a shop. After looking around, I would point to the thing I needed. Then I would ask its name in Spanish. By the time we left Monterey, my Spanish was quite good.

After a while, not as many people came out to the *Pilgrim* as before. The people of Monterey had done all their buying. It was time for us to leave. We set sail and started back for Santa Barbara.

This time, we had good sailing. Coming to Monterey from Santa Barbara took us almost three weeks. But going back took only one day. The next morning, we were there.

Everything looked just the same—the town, the hills without trees, the beach. Roaring waves were still breaking on the sand. As before, we anchored three miles out. We were the only ship there. The *Ayacucho* had left.

We had come back to Santa Barbara for hides. The men from the town had brought them down to the beach for us. But we would have to bring them out to the *Pilgrim*. It was our turn to do some "head work." We rowed in and looked over the hides. We made sure all the hides were dry. We would not take any that were still wet. Wet hides would go bad in the ship.

While we were in Santa Barbara, I learned how hides are dried. First, the hide is cut from the cow. Then two holes are cut in each end of it. These holes fit over the four posts in the ground. The posts keep the hide in place. They keep the hide from growing small as it dries in the sun.

We had seen how the men from the *Ayacucho* had carried the hides. But we thought we could find a better way. We did not want to carry them on our heads. We tried one way and then another. But not one of our ways was very good. After a short time, we started carrying them on our heads. That was the only way to keep them from getting splashed by the waves.

So that the hides would not hurt our heads, we took to wearing caps. The caps helped a lot. Getting the hides off the ground and up on our heads was quite a trick. In California, this is called "tossing a hide." The hides were heavy. And they were as wide as our arms were long. When the wind was strong, they were hard to pick up. Sometimes the wind would blow us off our feet. When this happened, we had to laugh at each other. Then we would get up and try again.

After a while, we learned the trick of "tossing a hide." Then we could fill our boats with hides in a short time. But it was always wet, hard work. We did not wear shoes because the water was bad for them. Our feet felt like ice. And they hurt from the

stones on the beach. When the boat was filled with
hides, our work was still not finished. We had to row
three miles back to the ship.

We carried hides all day long. We did not stop until the sun went down. By then, we were almost too
tired to stand up. We worked like horses. But nothing we did pleased Captain Thompson. He did not
think we were doing enough each day.

Captain Thompson was a hard-working man. I
never once saw him sit down. He was always busy,
always driving and pushing his men. He thought the
mate should be getting more work out of us.

The mate was a good man. He always did his work well. And he always made sure we sailors did everything right. But the mate was not like the captain. He was a quiet man. He did not push us in the same way the captain did.

After a while, the captain started giving orders himself. He watched us all the time. He never let us rest, not even for a minute. We thought Captain Thompson was driving us too hard. The captain knew how we felt. He could see it in our eyes. But this only made him push us even more. Day by day, he lost any liking he might have had for us.

All the time we were in Santa Barbara, the captain kept after us. From morning until night, we were busy tossing hides. Even when we got back to the ship at night, we could not rest. We had to stand watch. When it was time to go below, we fell asleep at once. We were too tired to do anything else.

From then on, all we did was work and sleep. There was no time to read or talk. We did not even have time to wash our clothes. But, at last, we had all the hides on board. We set sail and left Santa Barbara. We were on our way to San Pedro for more hides.

At sea, the captain still gave us no rest. Now, even when our watch was over, he would not let us go below. Rain or shine, he kept us on deck. I can still hear him telling us to "come up and see it rain."

It was not a happy ship that sailed into San Pedro.

7 The Whipping

San Pedro was not much more than a name.
There was no harbor. There was no town. Not a
house, not a building of any kind, could be seen. The
country was dry, brown, and without trees.

Still, we were told that this was the best place in
California to get hides. No one lived near the sea.
But not too many miles away was the town of Pueblo
de los Angeles. This town was bigger than any other
in California. All the hides from the town were
brought to San Pedro for shipping.

We filled our boat with cargo and rowed in. As we
got close, we could see that there was almost no
beach. A long, high hill came right down to the water.
As we landed, we saw a line of men coming over the
hill. They had come from Pueblo de los Angeles. The
men were bringing hides for our ship.

We pulled our boat up on the sand and looked at
the hill. What a hill! And we would have to carry all
the cargo to the top of it. We asked the men from the
town to help us. But all they did was smile and shake
their heads. This was our work, not theirs.

All day long, we carried cargo up the hill. Then,
when we were finished, we had to bring the hides
down. To save time, we threw the hides over the hill.
We let them slide down to the sand. It was night be-

fore we were done. We worked as fast as we could. But nothing we did seemed right or fast enough for Captain Thompson.

Then one day real trouble came. It was about ten in the morning. From below, we heard the sound of a man being hit. We heard the captain's voice. "Talk back to me, will you!" he cried.

There was no answer.

"Answer me!" the captain said.

"I have never talked back to you, Captain." It was a sailor we called Sam.

"That is not what I asked you!" the captain roared. "Will you ever talk back to me again?"

"I never have, Captain Thompson!" said Sam. "*I never have!*"

The captain came up on deck. There was fire in his eyes. He called out to the mate. "Take hold of that man, Mr. Amerzene!" he roared. "I'll whip him like a dog. I'll take the skin off him! Then you will all know who is captain of this ship. I'll teach you!"

The mate laid hold of Sam and pulled him on deck. Sam did not try to get away. But we could see that he was afraid.

Standing next to me was John the Swede. He was a good sailor. And he was always a friend to those in trouble. "Why are you going to whip that man, Captain?" he asked.

The captain pointed at John. "Take hold of him, too!" he said. One of the officers held John by the

arm. Then the mate tied Sam to the mast. He pulled off Sam's coat and stepped back.

The captain picked up a heavy rope. Swinging the rope over his head, he brought it down on Sam's back. The blow made a long, red cut.

We sailors were standing a few feet away. Watching this made me feel sick. To think that a man was being whipped like this!

Captain Thompson was hitting Sam as hard as he could. Six times he brought the rope down on Sam's back. "Will you ever talk back to me again?" he cried.

Sam did not answer.

Three more times the rope came down. This was too much. Sam said something, but we could not make out the words. The captain kept on whipping him. The man's back was covered with cuts.

At last, Captain Thompson stopped. "Take him below and put him back to work." Then he turned to John the Swede. "Now for you," the captain said.

But John had seen enough. He pulled away and started to run.

"Lay hold of him!" the captain cried. "Bring him back here and tie him to the mast!"

"Don't I do my work, Captain Thompson?" John asked. "Don't I work hard and work well?"

"Yes," Captain Thompson answered. "But I am not whipping you because of your work. I am whipping you because you asked me about Sam."

"Just for asking I get whipped?" John cried.

"Yes!" the captain roared. "No one shall open his mouth on board this ship but me."

Captain Thompson began laying blows on John's back. With each blow, the captain grew more wild. He danced about the deck, swinging the rope down on John again and again.

"So you want to know why I am whipping you!" he laughed. "Well, I'll tell you why. I am whipping you *because I feel like it!* It suits me! And on this

36

ship, I'll do anything I please! That is why I am whipping you!"

John could not take much more. "Oh, God! Help me. *Help me!*"

"Don't call on God!" roared the captain. "He can not help you. If you want help, *call on Frank Thompson*. He is the man. He is the only one who can help you!"

These words made me sick. I could look on no more. I turned my head away. But I could still hear the rope coming down on John's back.

At last, Captain Thompson ordered John cut down. Then the captain turned to us. He walked up and down the deck. "Now you see how it is!" he said. "Now you know who is the captain of this ship! You will do what I say, or I'll whip you all!" He kept on like this for another ten minutes. Then he left us.

I did not get much sleep that night. I kept thinking about what had happened. What kind of man was our captain? What right did he have to whip Sam and John? And what could we sailors do about it? I could not come up with any answers.

We stayed in San Pedro about a week. Captain Thompson worked us day and night. Down below, no one ever laughed or sang. We did not even talk much. We were beginning to think we would never see home again.

At last, we had all the hides on the ship that we could carry. We set sail and headed for San Diego.

8 A Man Runs Off

The *Pilgrim* moved along under full sail and soon we were off San Diego. The little harbor was at the mouth of a river. The opening to the harbor was not very wide. Only one ship at a time could sail into it.

There was a line of hills on one side of the harbor. On the other side was a wide sand beach. As in San Pedro, we could see no town. But not far from the beach, there were four large buildings that looked like barns. The buildings were hide-houses.

Three other ships were in the harbor. One of them was our old friend the *Ayacucho*. The names of the other two were the *Loriotte* and the *Lagoda*.

The *Pilgrim* sailed into the harbor heading right for the *Lagoda*. Captain Thompson was in too much of a hurry to be careful. He did not take in sail soon enough. At last, he called out, "All sail down! Let go the anchor!"

We did as the captain said. But the ship kept moving, pulling her anchor behind her. We could not stop her. We tried to turn. But before we could, the *Pilgrim* hit the *Lagoda* with a bang. We could hear boards breaking. There was a lot of noise, but the ships were not hurt much.

Captain Thompson could not get the *Pilgrim* away from the *Lagoda*. The bow of the *Pilgrim* was caught on the side of the other ship. He called out one order, then another. But nothing worked.

Then, all at once, the wind started blowing from the other way. The *Pilgrim* came away from the *Lagoda* by herself. But now she was moving straight for the *Ayacucho*. Captain Thompson gave still more orders. But we could not stop the ship. Our anchor would not hold.

Captain Wilson, of the *Ayacucho*, had been watching all this. He felt it was time to give us some help. His men put the *Ayacucho's* boat into the water and Captain Wilson came on board.

"Are you having a little trouble, Captain Thompson?" he asked.

"I think I can take care of it, Captain Wilson."

The captain of the *Ayacucho* smiled. He was a short, strong man. And he was an old hand at sailing a ship.

Captain Thompson gave us another order. "Oh, no," said Captain Wilson. "You don't want to do *that*. Will you let me help you?"

Soon, Captain Wilson was giving all the orders. First, he told us to pull up the anchor. We were more than happy to do what he said. Here, we thought, is a man who knows what he is doing. Captain Thompson stood by without saying a word.

In a few minutes, Captain Wilson had everything in order. We dropped our anchor again and the *Pilgrim* stopped. Then Captain Wilson got into his boat and left. We knew that Captain Thompson was glad to see him go. He did not like another man giving orders on his ship.

After dinner, the captain ordered two of us to row him over to the *Lagoda*. He wanted to talk to the *Lagoda's* captain. We brought our boat along side and Captain Thompson climbed on board. He told one of the *Lagoda's* sailors his name.

"Captain Thompson has come on board," the sailor called out to his captain.

"Did he come alone?" the *Lagoda's* captain answered. "Or did he bring his ship with him again?"

Captain Thompson did not find this at all funny. He grew red in the face. But we could not keep from laughing. Those words were a standing joke among us sailors from then on.

The next Sunday, I had my first real leave. The captain let all the sailors in our watch visit San Diego. The town was about three miles from the hidehouses. We washed from head to toe and put on our best clothes. When we were ready, we jumped into the boat. Because we were on leave, we did not even have to row. Sailors from the other watch did that.

I was with my friend Stimson. How good it felt to be away from the *Pilgrim* for a while. We had a full day to do what we pleased. We walked around town, looking at the shops and houses. We had a drink with some of the other sailors. Then we left them to walk around some more.

We wanted to go riding. But we did not know where we could get horses. After a while, we met a sailor from the *Ayacucho*. He knew San Diego well and soon found two horses for us.

We headed for the mission, three miles from town. After riding along for a while, we heard a bell ringing. We knew we were close. Soon we could see the mission buildings shining in the sun. They were made of mud and painted white. We tied up our horses and went inside the mission grounds.

One of the mission Fathers came out and said hello. We asked him if we could get something to eat. He said that we could. We followed him into a small room. There was nothing in it but a few pictures, a table, and three chairs. We sat down and talked with the Father in Spanish.

After a few minutes, an Indian boy came in. He brought us some baked meat and vegetables. Another boy came in with bread and fruit. I had not had such a good meal in a long time. When we fin-

ished, we left some money for the mission and said good-by.

We got on our horses and started back to the town. Off we went, racing along like the wind. Our horses loved to run. We felt as if we were flying. We kept on riding for most of the day. By the time night came, Stimson and I were both tired. We gave the horses back and went down to the beach. Our day of fun was over. It was time to go back to the ship.

By the end of the week, the *Pilgrim* was ready to leave San Diego. But before we sailed, the other sailors went into town for their day of leave. It was then that Foster got into trouble again.

Things had been bad for Foster. After breaking him as an officer, Captain Thompson had been pushing him hard. Nothing Foster did pleased him. Captain Thompson was out to get him.

Foster went into town with the other men. But he was late getting back to the ship that night. When he got back, Captain Thompson was waiting.

"You are late, Foster," the captain said. "I am going to teach you not to be late again." With those words, the captain picked up a rope.

Foster fell down on the deck. "Don't whip me, Captain!" he cried. "Please don't whip me!"

The captain looked at Foster as though he were a worm. He brought the rope down on the man's back a few times. But the blows were light. Then he sent Foster below.

The blows had not hurt Foster much. But he was afraid of what the captain would do next. That night, he put a boat into the water all by himself. Then, without making a sound, he rowed away. We knew he had gone, but we did not say anything.

The next morning, Captain Thompson saw that Foster was missing. He called all hands on deck. "Where is he? Where has that worm Foster gone?" he roared. "Some of you must have seen him leave!" But we would tell him nothing.

After breakfast, the captain went into town. He pulled a roll of money out of his pocket. And he said that the man who brought Foster back could have it. A lot of people wanted the money. They looked all over town for Foster. They even went into the hills on horses looking for him. But no one could find him.

The sailors from the *Lagoda* were hiding Foster. They had put him in one of the buildings near the beach. The men from the *Logoda* had heard about our captain. They knew what kind of man he was. Each day they brought Foster food and water. They told him he could stay until the *Pilgrim* sailed away.

At last, Captain Thompson gave up looking for Foster. We pulled up anchor and set sail for San Pedro again. We sailors had never liked Foster—as an officer or as a man. But we were glad he got away from Captain Thompson.

9 Curing Hides

By the time we left San Diego, we had sold most of our cargo. Now, there was room on the *Pilgrim* for more hides. First we went back to San Pedro. Then we moved on to Santa Barbara. At each place, we picked up hides. We did not get back to San Diego for five weeks.

When we got back, we started taking all the hides off the ship. We brought them into one of the four hide-houses near the beach. The hides were dry. But before we could bring them back to Boston, they had to be cured. Only cured hides can be used for making shoes and other things.

When all the hides were off the *Pilgrim*, Captain Thompson got ready to leave again. He was going out for more hides. But not all of us would be going along. Some of us were staying in San Diego. While the *Pilgrim* was away, we would begin curing the hides.

I stood on the sand and watched the *Pilgrim* sail away. Now I was a sailor without a ship—a land sailor. But that was all right. Living on the land for a while was fine with me.

Four of us were staying behind. Besides me, there were two other sailors, Henry and Nicholas. Henry, a boy from Marblehead, would do all the cooking.

Nicholas and I would work on the hides. There was also one officer, Mr. Russell.

The hide-house was our new home. It was quite a large building—the place could hold 40,000 hides. We lived in one corner of the building. Our room was small and dark. A little hole cut in the roof let in the only light. The floor was made of hard mud. The only things in the room were four beds, a table, and some cooking pans. Our officer, Mr. Russell, lived in a room of his own on the next floor.

I never saw a man bigger than Nicholas. He was more than six feet tall. His feet were so large he could not find shoes in California to fit him. And he was as strong as a horse. Nicholas had been a sailor from the time he was a boy. He had never learned how to read or write.

We always got along very well together. He knew that I had been to Harvard College. Because of that, he thought great things were in store for me.

"I'll be good friends with you," he used to say. "You are on the way up. By and by, you will come out here a captain on your own ship. Then I'll call you *Captain* Dana. But you and I will still be friends. You will not be hard on your old friend Nicholas." I told him I did not want to be a captain. But Nicholas would never believe it.

Nicholas and I were not the only men working on the hides. Captain Thompson was paying four sailors from the Sandwich Islands to help us. I came to like these men very much. They were as nice as people could be.

One of the Sandwich Islanders was a man we called Tom Davis. He knew some English. The other three knew only their own language. I liked Tom and used to joke with him all the time. But Hope was the man I liked best. Even though Hope did not know English, we became great friends. I learned a little of his language, and soon we could talk together.

I wanted to know all about the Sandwich Islands. Hope did his best to tell me. Sometimes he drew pictures in the sand with a stick. He told me about his family, his friends, and the ways of his people.

Hope wanted to know about my home, too. I told him about Boston and about some of the other American cities. He could not read. But he loved to look at the pictures in the books I had.

One day, he saw a picture of a train. Hope had never seen anything like it before. There were no trains in the Sandwich Islands. He wanted to know how a train works. Knowing only a little of his language, I did not think I could do it. But Hope was quick to catch on. He had no trouble learning almost anything.

The day the *Pilgrim* left, we began curing the hides. As I said, the hides were dry when we got them. They were as hard as boards. Before we could cure them, we had to make the hides soft again.

First, we took the hides down to the sea and put them in the water. We tied them down so that the waves would not wash them away. After two days in the sea, the hides became soft. Then we brought them back to the hide-house.

Near the hide-house, we kept large pans of water cooking over a fire. The water was full of salt. We put the soft skins into the water and then threw in more salt. It was the salt that did the curing. After the hides had cooked in the water for two days, they were cured. Because of the salt, they would not go bad.

But the hides were still not ready. Next, we took the cooked hides and put them on the ground. We cut off bits of meat and fat that were still on the hides. We also cut off the ear and leg pieces. They could not be used for anything. We had to work with care. If we cut off too little, the work had to be done over. If we cut off too much, we would have trouble from Mr. Russell.

Curing hides was hard work. Our backs and legs hurt all the time. And the hides smelled bad. The smell was strong enough to make you sick. But we still thought it was better than being on the *Pilgrim* with Captain Thompson.

We were not the only people curing hides in San Diego. There were men working in the other three hide-houses as well. Some, like us, were from the United States. Others, like Tom Davis and Hope, were from the Sandwich Islands. Still others came from Italy, France, and Spain. Two men were from England. One was from Ireland and another from Holland. We even had two men from Chile and one from Tahiti.

Soon, we all knew one another. At night, we would get together to smoke and tell stories. Sometimes, some of the men would sing. I heard songs from almost every country in almost every language.

The days skipped by, one after another. After six weeks, we had finished curing all the hides in our hide-house. They were ready to go to Boston. But the *Pilgrim* had still not come back. For once, there was not much for us to do.

When we were cooking the hides, we had a fire going day and night. The pans of water had to be kept hot. We had used up a lot of wood. Now, our wood was almost gone. The *Pilgrim* would be back soon with more hides. We would need more wood then. This was a good time, we thought, to get some.

Every day for the next week, we looked for wood. Each morning, we would go up into the hills. We had to walk a long way to find wood. All the trees near the hide-houses had been cut down. Even a mile away, there were no big trees. Most of them were only five or six feet high.

The little trees grew close together, like weeds. It was hard to cut them down. The branches kept sticking us and making holes in our clothes. But by the end of the week, we had all the wood we needed.

At last, on July 8, the *Pilgrim* came back to San Diego. We were surprised to learn that Captain Thompson was not on board. He had left the *Pilgrim* to take over as captain of another ship, the *Alert*.

The *Pilgrim's* new captain was a man named Edward Faucon. After the ship had anchored, he came to see us in the hide-house. Captain Faucon was a short, dark man with smiling eyes. I could tell right away that he was not at all like Captain Thompson. He would never think of hitting a man with a rope.

Captain Faucon looked around the hide-house. "Good work, men," he told us. "You have done your work well. Which one of you is Dana?"

"I am, Captain."

"I have a box for you from Boston," Captain Faucon said. "It is on the ship. Come on board after dinner and get it."

About seven that night, I rowed out to the *Pilgrim* to get the box. I also wanted to say hello to my old friends. I was glad to see Stimson again. It was also good to see John the Swede and Sam once more.

"How do you like your new captain?" I asked.

"Captain Faucon is one of the best," Sam answered. "He is as good a man as Captain Thompson is bad."

"And how do you like working on the hides?" Stimson asked.

"It is all right," I said, "once you get used to the smell."

We talked until the next watch began. Then I took my box and rowed back to the beach. The box was from my family. It was filled with new clothes. They had come just in time. All my old clothes were full of holes.

On top of the clothes, tied with a string, were ten letters. I was glad to get the clothes. But the letters pleased me even more. It was great to have news from home. I sat up almost all night reading them. When I finished, I read them again.

10 The *Alert*

For the next three days, we did nothing but carry hides off the *Pilgrim*. The ship was filled with them. But we still had a long way to go before the hide-house was filled. And we knew we could not go back to Boston until then.

On July 11, the *Pilgrim* left again. We stayed behind to cure the hides she had brought. For the next seven weeks, we worked on them. Every afternoon, when our work was done, we looked for the *Alert*. We had heard she would be coming to San Diego. And all of us wanted to see her.

I wanted to see the *Alert* more than anyone. When I signed on the *Pilgrim*, I had planned to be away only two years. But now, the *Pilgrim* was going to stay in California another year. That was why Captain Faucon took over from Captain Thompson. The *Alert* was going back to Boston first.

My eyes were better now, and I wanted to get back to Harvard. I wrote my family saying that I wished to come back on the *Alert*. In Boston, my father went to see the men who owned the ship. They sent Captain Thompson a letter. He was told to let me sail on the *Alert*.

At long last, the *Alert* sailed in to San Diego. As soon as the sailors came off the ship, I went over to them. If I sailed on the *Alert*, another sailor would have to take my place. There were still a lot of hides that needed curing. I soon found a man who was willing to work in the hide-house. He was tired of sailing and wanted to live on land for a while. The two of us went to see Captain Thompson.

"Well, what do you want?" he said.

"I would like to sail on the *Alert*, Captain," I answered. "This man wants to take my place in the hide-house."

Captain Thompson looked at the man. "Don't you like working on my ship?" he asked the man.

"Oh, yes, I do," the sailor answered. "But I would like to try my hand at curing hides."

"All right, Dana," said the captain. "Get your things and come on board."

The next day, I said good-by to my friends and boarded the *Alert*. This ship was much bigger than the *Pilgrim*. There were many more sailors on board. But there was room enough for every man. I liked the *Alert*. Everything was as clean as could be. The forecastle was bright and shining. It was not at all like the *Pilgrim*.

Even Captain Thompson was not the same. On the *Pilgrim*, he thought the mate was too soft. Because of this, he had started giving orders himself. But he liked the mate on the *Alert*. Most of the time, we never saw Captain Thompson. He let the mate give the orders.

We sailors liked the mate, too. Mr. Brown had a voice like a lion. He never had to give an order more than once. But we were not afraid of him. He was a good man. And we did our best to please him.

Mr. Brown put me on the night watch. That was how I met Tom Harris. I have never met anyone like Tom Harris. Even though he had not finished school, he could think rings around me. Tom could look at a ship and tell how many hides it would hold. He did not even need a piece of paper. He worked everything out in his head.

Tom did not need to write things down. He remembered everything. He remembered the name of every ship he had worked on. He remembered the day it had sailed and the day it got back. And, what is more, he remembered the name of every man on board:

"After I left the *Danford*, I signed on the *Towanda*. She left Boston on July 6, 1827. That was a Tuesday. Captain Lawson had five men on board. Besides me, there was Ned Jones, Peter Wood, 'Bear' Wilson, and Billy the Scot. We were gone two years and three weeks to the day. We brought back 28,640 hides."

Tom and I became good friends. He told me all about himself. His father had been the captain of a small ship. He was killed when Tom was still a small boy. Tom's mother did her best. But Tom was a wild boy. He left school and ran off to sea.

Now, he knew he had not done the right thing. If he had stayed in school, he could have been an officer. He might even have become a captain. "Look at me, Dana," Tom said one day. "All these years at sea, and I am still just a sailor. My trunk in the forecastle is all I can show for it. A trunk full of old clothes!"

The *Alert* sailed north to San Juan for more hides. The country around San Juan is beautiful. A rock cliff comes straight up from the beach. There is only one way to the top. The *Pilgrim* had stopped here once, so I knew the way. Captain Thompson told me to climb up and get the hides.

It took quite a while to get to the top. I rested for a minute and then began to work. First I counted the hides. Then I started throwing them over the cliff. That was the only way to get the hides to the beach. It was a long way down. The men walking about on the sand looked as small as bugs. As the hides landed, the men picked them up and put them in our boat.

I worked all day. At last, there were no more hides to throw. I climbed down to the beach thinking I had done my work well. But Captain Thompson was not happy. About ten hides were caught on the side of the cliff. He would not leave without them.

I went back up the cliff with another man. We had a long rope with us. He tied one end of it to a tree. He threw the other end over the cliff.

"Make sure the rope stays tied!" I told him.

"I will," he answered. "And *you* make sure you hold on."

"I'll do that!"

Holding the rope, I climbed down, hand over hand. Below, there was nothing but thin air. If I fell, I knew I would be killed.

After about five minutes, I got to the place where the hides were caught. Holding on with one hand, I pulled at them. The rope was swinging in the wind. But I kept on working. One by one, the hides dropped to the sand. At last, I finished and climbed down to the beach.

I thought Captain Thompson would thank me for getting the hides. But he just laughed at me. "You looked like a monkey," he said.

11 A Party in Santa Barbara

The *Alert* left San Juan on October 20. We visited San Pedro and Santa Barbara again. Then we moved on to San Francisco. The sun was shining when we got there. But rain started to fall the next day. It rained without stopping for three weeks. We had a hard time keeping the hides dry. At last, they were all on board and we left San Francisco.

On January 10, we were back in Santa Barbara. The day was bright and warm. We could not have come at a better time. The people of the town were getting ready for a big party.

Donna Anita was going to be married. Her father, Don Antonio, was the head of the first family in California. He asked all the officers and sailors from the *Alert* to come to the party.

Captain Thompson sent our cook to Don Antonio's house. The cook stayed there three days baking pies and cakes for the party. At last the day came when Donna Anita was to be married. We had all the ship's flags flying. Then we put on our best clothes and went into town.

People from all over California had come to see Donna Anita get married. Donna Anita was a beautiful woman. Her hair was long and black, and her eyes were deep brown. As she came by, the people began waving and calling out their best wishes.

That night, the party began. There were colored lights all around Don Antonio's house. Music filled the air. All the men, women, and children of the town were there. Even the poor people were dressed in fine, bright-colored clothes. Many people were dancing and singing. Others, like me, were happy just to watch.

This party was not at all like parties I had been to in Boston. The people played games I had never seen before. Before a party, women fill chicken eggs with flower water. They make a small hole in each end of the egg. They blow out the egg and fill it with sweet-smelling water.

The women bring baskets of these party eggs with them. When a man is not looking, a woman comes up behind him. She breaks an egg on his head. Then she runs off before he can see who did it. All the people laugh. No one will tell the man who hit him with the egg. He must try to find her on his own. When he does, he breaks an egg on her head. But he, too, must do it when the woman is not looking.

As I was watching the dancing, Donna Augustia came up to me. She was Donna Anita's sister. Donna Augustia smiled and asked me to move to one side. She had a party egg in her hand. In front of us, his back turned, was her uncle Don Domingo. Donna Augustia came up behind him, as quiet as a mouse.

Down came the egg! Don Domingo turned to see who had hit him. But the girl was gone. Flower water was running down his face. We all laughed at the joke. Don Domingo had to laugh, too.

The men from the *Alert* were having a great time, eating, drinking, and dancing. Then, about ten that night, Captain Thompson said it was time to leave. Going back to the ship, we all felt good. We had not had such fun for a long time.

We left Santa Barbara the next day. In about a week, we were back in San Diego. I was always glad to see San Diego. Having worked there all summer, the place seemed like home to me. As soon as the hides were off the ship, I went to see my friends.

They were happy to see me again. But I found my good friend Hope was quite sick. He looked very bad.

Hope lay on his bed with his eyes closed. It was hard for him to talk. The other Sandwich Islanders had tried to help. But there was nothing they could do. They had no medicine. I knew that if something was not done soon, he would never get well.

The next morning, I went to see Captain Thompson. I told him how sick Hope was. I thought that he would be glad to help.

"What! Take time to help a Sandwich Islander?" he said. "Why should I? I don't care if he lives or not."

"But Captain," I said, "he has worked for years curing hides for you."

"That counts for nothing. I don't have enough medicine as it is. I will not throw it away on him!" With that, the captain turned his back and walked away.

I did not know what to do next. Then I remembered a sailor on the *Alert* called Old Mike. Old Mike had been a sailor for a great many years. He had seen almost everything. I thought that he might help.

The next day, Old Mike and I went to the hide-house. When he saw Hope, he turned to me shaking his head. "I have seen a lot of sick men in my time," he said. "But I have never seen anyone as sick as this who lived."

"Can you help him?" I asked.

"I'll do what I can," answered Old Mike. "Many years ago I learned how to make a strong drink from roots. That may help him."

Old Mike opened a little bag he had with him. Inside were some dried roots. He took a few out and ground them up between his hands. Then he put the ground roots in a cup of hot water.

"Drink this," he told the Sandwich Islander. It did not smell very good. But Hope tried to drink it all. After a while, he said he felt better. He told us he was glad his friends cared about him. *That* made him feel better than any medicine, he said. But I knew he had to have medicine. And he had to have it soon.

I visited Hope as often as I could. He kept saying that he felt better. But he did not look any better. About that time, the *Pilgrim* sailed in. As soon as I could, I went to see Captain Faucon. I asked him if he could help my poor friend.

"I know Hope," Captain Faucon said. "He once worked for me. He is a good man, and I would like to help him. But I have no medicine to give him."

"Is there nothing you can do?" I asked.

"The *California* will be here in a week," Captain Faucon answered. "I know the captain of that ship well. He is sure to have the medicine Hope needs. When he gets to San Diego, I'll talk to him. I know he will be glad to help."

12 The Captain's Trick

The hide-house was now filled with hides. At last, we were ready to start back to Boston. But first, we had to clean out the ship. We carried everything off. Then we filled some pans with wet tree bark and set fire to them. We put the pans below and closed up the ship. Heavy blue smoke filled the inside of the *Alert*. When we opened the ship again, all the bugs and mice had been killed.

Now we could start bringing the hides on board. 40,000 hides! I did not believe we could get them all in. We worked for six weeks, stopping only to eat and sleep. We brought hide after hide on board. There seemed to be no end to them. We pushed and pressed the hides into every open place. At last, we had every one on board.

I was glad that the time had come to leave. But I kept thinking about Hope. He was still living. But every day looked like his last. The *California* was seven weeks late. I wondered if Hope could be saved.

Then one morning I heard the cry, "Ship coming in!" It was the *California*. I stood on deck and watched her sail in. The *California* looked like a happy ship. Her men were singing as they worked.

While I was watching, a sailor told me Captain Thompson wanted to see me. I followed the sailor below. There I found Captain Thompson. Captain Faucon was with him.

Captain Thompson turned to me with a funny smile on his face. "Well, Dana," he said, "so you think you are going home on the *Alert*."

"Yes, Captain," I answered. "You know that is my plan."

"What do I care about your plan?" Captain Thompson said. "You signed on the *Pilgrim*. Now you want to sail on the *Alert*. Is there a sailor from the *Alert* who will take your place? If not, you can not go with us. You will have to go back on the *Pilgrim*."

What could I do? The sailor who took my place in the hide-house wanted to go home. He did not want to stay behind and work on the *Pilgrim* for another year.

What Captain Thompson was doing was not right. He had orders from Boston to let me sail on the *Alert*. He had even told me that I could go with him. Now he was springing this trick on me. And he had waited until just before the *Alert* was leaving to tell me. He knew I would have a hard time finding a man to take my place. Not one sailor on the *Alert* wanted to stay another day in California.

"Captain Thompson," I said, "I have a right to sail on the *Alert*. I know you have orders from Boston to take me. My family sent me a letter telling me so."

The captain looked at me like a wolf looks at a rabbit. But I was not afraid of him. I had to stand up to him. I told him again that I had a right to sail on the *Alert*. Captain Thompson said nothing. He knew that my family could make trouble for him. And now, Captain Faucon knew about the orders from Boston. Captain Thompson had to back down.

"Very well, Dana," he said. "I'll find a sailor to

take your place. Get back to work. And send Ben down here."

Captain Thompson told Ben that he would have to sail on the *Pilgrim*. Ben was a poor boy from England. He did not want to stay in California another year. But there was nothing he could do. The other sailors did not like this at all.

"It is all right for you," a sailor said to me. "You have a fine family to watch out for you. Nothing is going to happen to *you*. But who will watch out for Ben? Because of you, he has to stay behind."

Up to this point, I had got along well with the men on the *Alert*. I had worked as hard as anyone. And I was as much of a sailor as any man. But now, the others were beginning to feel that I was not one of them. It was up to me to do something.

I told the men I would give money to anyone who would take my place.

"There is not enough money in the world to make *me* stay," said one man.

"What good is money out here?" said another. "There is nothing to buy."

But at last I found a sailor who would do it. He was a boy from Boston we called Harry Bluff. "I'll take your place," said Harry. "I don't care if I see Boston this year or next. If there is enough money in it for me, I'll stay."

So Captain Thompson's trick did not work after all. Everything turned out all right. Ben stayed on the *Alert*. Harry got his money. And I got to go back to Boston.

Before we left, I found time to see Captain Arthur on board the *California*. I asked him if he could help my friend Hope.

"Captain Faucon has already told me about Hope," he answered."I have some medicine that I think will help him." The captain went to his trunk and got out the medicine. Then he came with me to the hide-house.

When Hope saw us come in, he tried to stand up. But he was not strong enough. Captain Arthur told him to rest. He gave him the medicine. He told Hope to take some every day until he felt better. Hope thanked the captain for coming to see him. I thanked him, too.

I went to see Hope once more before the *Alert* left. He was already beginning to get well. We talked for a while. Then I said good-by to my friend. The *Alert* was about to sail.

The deck of our ship looked like a farm. We had four cows, ten sheep, ten pigs, and some chickens on board. We brought the animals along so that we could have fresh meat on our trip.

That afternoon, Captain Thompson told us to set sail. How long we had waited to hear those words! We were leaving California at last.

Because of all the hides on board, the *Alert* was slow in starting. Her bottom was far down in the water. It seemed almost as though she were not moving at all.

We neared the mouth of the harbor. Ahead of us was the wide blue sea. Then, all at once, there was a jarring bump. The ship stopped.

The water at the mouth of the harbor was not deep. The *Alert* had no trouble sailing into the harbor. She was not filled with hides then. But now, with all the hides on board, the *Alert* could not get out. She was caught in the mud.

Captain Thomspon walked up and down, trying to think of something to do. But there was nothing he *could* do. The mud on the bottom of the harbor had us. We were rooted there like a tree.

"Keep an eye on the wind, Mr. Brown," Captain Thompson said. "And be ready to put out more sail."

The wind was light. But if a strong wind began to blow, it could carry us off the mud. We all waited. The sun went down and night came. By this time, we had thought we would be far out to sea. But here we were, still in the harbor.

At last, late that night, a strong wind began to blow. Mr. Brown told us to put up every sail we had. The wind filled the sails. But for a minute nothing happened. Then, we could feel the *Alert* beginning to move.

Before long, we were in deep water. We were still not moving very fast. But we *were* moving. The *Alert* was on her way home.

13 Hard Sailing

For the first few weeks, the days were bright and warm. But we knew that such days would soon end. We were heading for Cape Horn. And it would be winter when we got there.

We knew we would have a hard time getting around the Cape. Because of all the hides on board, the *Alert* was very low in the water. In a storm, the waves would wash over her from end to end. The *Alert* was a strong ship. But we wondered if she would be strong enough.

On top of this, we were short-handed. Captain Thompson had worked the men too hard in California. Carrying hides to and from the ship was killing work. We were wet most of the time. And we never had time to rest. Because of this, some of the men became sick. We had to leave one man behind. He was too sick to sail with us. And another man, Henry Mellus, was too sick to do any work on board.

The days became cold. The sky was still blue. But the sun did little to warm us. We put on our heavy clothes and did our best to keep out the cold. We were still a long way from Cape Horn, but we had already left summer behind.

One morning, the wind began to spring up. We knew we were in for a storm. The waves became bigger and bigger. The *Alert* met them head-on. But she had a hard time riding over them. She was too low in the water.

All morning the wind blew strong. By afternoon, great waves were banging into the ship. Each wave made the ship shake as if she had run into a rock.

At four, my watch was called. I got dressed and went up on deck. Just then, I saw a wave as big as a house coming at us. I was sailor enough to know that the *Alert* could not ride over this wave. I could tell by the "feeling of her" under my feet.

If I did not do something fast, I would be washed over the side. Springing up on the rigging, I held on with all my might. The wave came rolling down on the ship with a roar. It almost knocked me from the rigging. For a minute, everything was under water.

The wave washed almost everything on deck over the side. Most of the animals were gone. Only six sheep were left. They stood there, cold, wet, and too afraid to move.

The galley was gone, too. All that was left of it were some boards. Two men had been in the galley when the wave hit. At first, we thought they had been washed over the side.

"Where is the cook?" said Mr. Brown. "And where is Bill? He was in the galley, too."

Then we heard a voice from under the boards. "Get me out of here!" It was the cook.

"And give me a hand, too," said another voice.

"Is that you, Bill?" asked a sailor.

"Who do you think it is, your grandmother?" Bill answered.

We pulled the boards away and helped the two men get up. The men were wet, but not hurt.

"I tell you," said Bill, "we will never make it around the Cape. The ship can not even ride over *these* waves. And Cape Horn waves are much bigger. I don't think we can do it. The *Alert* is just too low in the water."

But the cook laughed at him. "Why don't you tell that to the sheep? They are afraid, too."

"You saw what that wave did to us," Bill said. "I tell you, we will all be killed. The *Alert* will never get around Cape Horn."

"Sure she will," answered the cook. "This is nothing but a little joke the sea played on us. We just got a little wet. No one is going to get killed."

By the next morning, the storm was over. But we knew that this was just the first of many storms we would see. For the next few days, we worked hard putting up new ropes and sails. We wanted to be ready for the next storm.

One morning, I woke up with a toothache. At first, it did not hurt much. I thought it would soon go away. But the next day my tooth hurt even more. I asked Mr. Brown if he had any medicine for a toothache. But most of the medicine was gone. There was nothing he could give me.

As if this was not enough, another storm came up. Heavy rain began to fall, and the wind blew hard. The cold air made my tooth hurt even more.

Day after day, the storm went on. My tooth hurt so much that I could not sleep at nights. When I had to be on watch, I was almost too tired to stand up. And working in the cold rain did not make me feel any better.

My face became puffed up like a balloon. One morning, I could not even open my mouth enough to eat. The cook asked Captain Thompson if he could make some soup for me.

"No!" cried the captain. "Tell him to eat salt meat and hard bread like the rest of the men."

The mate, Mr. Brown, heard what Captain Thompson told the cook. Mr. Brown was a kind man. That afternoon, he brought the cook some soft vegetables. "Make the boy some soup," Mr. Brown said to the cook. "But don't let Captain Thompson know about this."

The soup made me feel better for a while. But by night, my toothache was as bad as ever. I seemed to hurt all over. I had never felt so bad before.

If there had been more men on board, I could have rested. But we were short-handed. We were not far from the Cape now, and we needed every man on deck.

I did my best to keep working. But I was too sick to be of much help to the others. One morning, as I went to stand my watch, Mr. Brown called me over. "Go below, Dana," he said, "and climb into your bunk. You are too sick to be up here."

I did as he said. And I knew he was right. I was so sick I almost did not make it back to my bunk. The bad tooth felt like a red-hot nail in my face. But I was so tired that I was soon asleep. The next morning, I felt a little better. But I was still not strong enough to do any work.

I could feel the ship rocking and shaking in the storm. Wave after wave rolled down on her. Then I heard Captain Thompson call all hands together. I could hear his voice over the wind. "I want every man to stay on deck," he said. "We will need every man to keep the *Alert* from going down."

I knew that I had to do my part, too. I got out of my bunk and started putting my clothes on. Everything seemed to be going around before my eyes. Then, I turned and saw Mr. Brown.

"What do you think you are doing?" he said.

"I heard what Captain Thompson told the men," I answered. "I am coming up to help."

"Get back into that bunk!" Mr. Brown said. "If the *Alert* goes down, we will all go down together. Being up on deck will not save you or anyone else. But if you go out in that cold air, you may never see Boston again."

I got back into my bunk. But I could not sleep. To a sailor, nothing is quite as bad as being sick in a storm. He wants to help, but knows he can do nothing. And he knows that by being sick, he makes more work for the others. The other sailors must stand his watch until he is better.

After two more days, the storm ended. I was still not strong enough to get out of bed. But in another day, I felt better and came up on deck. I was surprised at what I saw.

The *Alert* looked as though she were made of ice, not wood. Ice covered everything. There was ice in the water, too. Great pieces of ice were all around the ship. Some of them were as big as our ship. Had we hit one of these in the storm, the *Alert* would have gone down.

I walked over to the side and looked out at the ice. Getting around Cape Horn was hard enough. With all this ice in the way, I wondered if we would make it after all. Only time would tell.

14 Fields of Ice

Ice was all around the *Alert*. The sea was full of it. Some pieces were small. But others were as large as the ship. We sailed along, looking for a way around the ice. But there were fields of ice as far as we could see. At last, Captain Thompson turned the *Alert* west, away from Cape Horn. We sailed for many days before heading for the Cape again.

I was on watch with Bill, the sailor who was almost washed over the side. "It looks like we will never get around Cape Horn," he said. "This makes three times now that we have tried to get around the ice."

"Three times?" I asked.

"Yes," he said. "We first tried when you were sick. But there was too much ice. We had to go back. We tried again after you came back to work. And now we are trying still again. That makes three times."

"Do you think we will make it this time?" I asked.

"Not if another storm hits us, I don't," he answered. "That ice will break this ship in two."

Bill was a man who always looked on the dark side of things. But I wondered if he might be right this time. We were near Cape Horn again. The sky was cold and gray. The wind was beginning to blow, and you could almost feel a storm in the air. But we still had not seen any ice. I was glad about that.

That afternoon, when my watch was over, I went below to get some sleep. If a storm was coming, I wanted to have all the rest I could get. I could feel the ship rocking up and down in the waves. But I was soon asleep.

I had not been sleeping long when I heard Captain Thompson's voice. "All hands on deck! And be quick about it! Don't stop for your coats!"

I jumped to my feet and raced up on deck with the others. There, just in front of the ship, was an iceberg. In another minute, we would run into it.

"Bring her about!" said Mr. Brown to the man at the wheel. "Turn her hard!"

With all the ropes and rigging covered with ice, the ship was slow in turning. We were still heading for the iceberg. But, at last, the ship turned away, missing the ice by only a few feet.

I could see icebergs all around us. There was more ice than ever. Winding our way between so much ice would be hard. And, as if this was not bad enough, night was coming.

Captain Thompson called us together. "We will need more than one look-out," he said. "I want every man to stay on deck until morning. Keep your eyes open and watch out for the ice."

It was a long night. We had look-outs on every part of the deck. When a look-out spotted an iceberg, he cried out, "Ice off the bow!" Moving fast, the man at the wheel turned the ship out of the way. The rest of us pulled the sails up or down to catch the wind right. We were at it all night. As soon as we got around one iceberg, another would be spotted.

We were all tired. It seemed that morning would never come. It was hard to see the icebergs in the dark night. On top of this, it began to snow. At times, we could not see anything at all. For all we knew, we could have been headed right for an iceberg.

At last, the sky began to get light in the east. Morning had come. The snow stopped and soon the sun was shining in the cold blue sky. Now we could see where we were going.

By that afternoon, the *Alert* was in open water

again. There were only a few icebergs here and there. The ice fields were behind us. But we still had to get around Cape Horn.

On we sailed. A good wind was blowing, and the *Alert* moved along, mile after mile. All at once, the look-out called out at the top of his voice, "*Sail!* Sail coming up!"

Those were glad words. We had not seen another ship from the time we left San Diego. Even Captain Thompson seemed pleased. Those of us not on watch ran to the side. We looked for the ship, but all we saw was the sea. Then, as we were standing there, the look-out called out again. "Another sail coming up!" he said. "There are two of them!"

To come upon another ship down here at the world's end was surprising. But to see *two* other ships was hard to believe. We looked for the ships, but saw nothing. Mr. Brown called out to the look-out. "I don't see anything," he said. "Where are they?"

After a minute, the look-out said, "I guess they are not sails after all. It must be land I see."

"Land, my eye!" Mr. Brown answered. "You spotted two icebergs, nothing more!" A few more minutes of sailing showed that he was right. The icebergs were off to one side of us, about two miles away. They were not in our way, and we sailed on.

It was a beautiful day. The sun was bright. And the sea was a deep blue. The *Alert* moved along, her sails full of wind.

"If this wind keeps up," I said, "we will soon be around Cape Horn."

"Don't count on it," said Bill. "Cape Horn may still have a trick or two for us."

Bill was right this time. Just before dark, the wind stopped blowing. Without wind, we could not sail another foot. The sails dropped down around the mast, and the *Alert* stopped. We sat there, not moving at all. It looked as though we were in for a quiet night.

But then, all at once, the wind began blowing again. And what wind! It roared in our ears, sounding like all the tigers in the world. This was the father of all storms. Snow flew in the air and great waves washed over the ship. We took in all the sails.

But even with her sails down, the *Alert* could not stand up to the storm. The wind pushed her back, blowing her away from Cape Horn. It seemed as though the Cape were saying, "No, you don't. You shall not get around Cape Horn. Back you go!"

For more than a week, it was like this. One minute, there would be no wind at all. The next minute, driving winds would push us away from the Cape. We tried as hard as we could to sail east. But the wind kept pushing us west.

And it was so cold! The sky was gray and dark all day long. The sun seemed to be lost for good. Snow fell most of the time. It was so heavy we could not see our hands in front of our eyes.

When it was not snowing, it was raining. The rain was as cold as ice. There was no way to stay dry. Every man on board was soon wet to the skin. And all our clothes were wet, too.

Each day was the same—snow, rain, and wind; snow, rain, and wind. At night, it was almost too cold to sleep. And we had no dry clothes to put on. Time seemed to stop. One minute seemed like two. One day seemed like a week.

We felt Cape Horn was playing with us like a cat plays with a mouse. No matter how long the game lasts, the cat stays as strong as ever. But the mouse gets more and more tired. And then the cat ends the game—by killing the mouse. We knew that Cape Horn was the cat. And the *Alert* was the mouse.

Cape Horn was wearing us out. When we tried to go east, the wind pushed us west. As soon as we put up our sails, a storm would make us take them down. We began to think we would never get around the Cape.

All we did was work and sleep. No one felt much like talking. There was nothing to say. The only thing we ever talked about at all was getting back home. But we had stopped saying "*when* we get home." Now, we were saying "*if* we get home."

15 Talking to the Ship

Day after day, the wind, the snow, and the cold kept on. We could not take much more of it. Some of the men were sick and could not work. The rest of us were so tired that we almost could not stand. And to top it off, we were not even sure quite where we were. The driving winds had pushed the *Alert* miles from where she should have been.

We still kept trying to get around Cape Horn. Most of the time, the wind tried to blow us away from the Cape. But now and then, it blew from the west. When it did, we put up all the sails. But we could never keep them up for long. A storm would always make us take them down.

Little by little, the *Alert* moved on. One night, while I was on watch, a storm came up. The wind pulled at the sails. It was blowing strong and wild.

Mr. Brown looked up at the sails. He saw that they could not stand up before the storm. They would have to come down. In this storm, all of the men would be needed to do the work. Mr. Brown cupped his hands to call the others on deck. But Captain Thompson stopped him.

"We must let the sailors down below get some rest," he told Mr. Brown. "If we don't, they will be too tired to be of any use to us. Let the men on watch tie down the sails."

This was bad news for us. Our watch was short-handed. Two of the men were sick. And another man had cut his hand and could not work. There were only six of us on deck. One sailor had to stay at the wheel. That left only five men to tie down the sails.

With so few of us, we could only work on one sail at a time. We had to work with great care. Everything was covered with ice. If anyone fell into the sea, he would be lost for sure. No one could swim in that cold water.

We had a hard time getting the sails tied down. The wind kept pulling them from our hands. Then the cold began to get to us. After a while, I lost all feeling in my hands. I could not keep hold of anything. I clapped my hands together as hard as I could to get them warm. The feeling came back to them for a short time. Then it was gone again. Every few minutes, I had to stop to warm my hands.

We worked as fast as we could. But it was a long time before we got all the sails tied in place. At last, we were finished. Just as we were climbing down, the bell rang ending our watch. The sound of that bell was music to our ears. We lost no time going below. We pulled off our wet clothes and fell into our bunks. In a minute, every man was asleep.

The next morning, the sky was still dark and gray. But the storm had ended. The *Alert* moved along with a good wind in her sails. Then, that afternoon, the sun came out. Every man on board was glad to see it. We had not had any sunshine for weeks. It seemed like a good sign.

Just then, the look-out called out. "*Land!*" he cried. "Land off the bow!"

The words were hard to believe. Was it land this time? Or was it nothing but more ice? I ran up on deck as soon as I could. Sure enough, there was land. It was so far away, I almost could not see it. But I could tell that it was not ice. It was real land.

"What land is that?" asked Mr. Brown.

"It must be Staten Island," answered Captain Thompson.

"Then we must be around Cape Horn," said Mr. Brown. "We are on the Boston side of the Cape now."

A sailor named Jack jumped into the air. "We made it!" he cried. "*We made it!*" There was a smile on every man's face. We began to think we would get home after all.

"Head her north!" said Captain Thompson. "Nothing can stop us now."

We all wanted to get to Boston as soon as we could. But I think Captain Thompson was in more of a hurry than anyone else. He got married just before leaving Boston. For two long years now, he had not seen the woman he was married to.

Captain Thompson could not keep still for a minute. He walked up and down, keeping a close eye on everything. He did everything he could to make the *Alert* sail as fast as she could.

"Mr. Brown!" he said. "Put up more sail! What she can not carry let her pull along behind!"

"What does the captain think he is doing?" said one of the men. "We already have as much sail up as she can hold. The ship can not take any more without something breaking."

But we had to do as the captain said. We climbed up the masts and put up more sails. Then we hurried back down. If a mast was going to break, we did not want to be on it.

The sails were pulling hard on the ropes. And a funny sound was coming from the masts. It was as though the pulling hurt them and they were crying. Any minute now, I thought, something is going to break. And still Captain Thompson called for more sail.

But everything held. The *Alert* raced along like an arrow. With so many sails up, her bow was pulling up out of the water. It seemed as though the ship were springing across the sea.

When my trick at the wheel came, I could not hold the wheel alone. The ship was as hard to turn as a wild horse. It took two of us working with all our might to steer her.

Mr. Brown was pleased with the way the *Alert* was sailing. He stood there rubbing his hands together and talking to the ship. "Hurry up, old girl," he said. "You know where you are going, don't you? The Boston girls have got hold of your ropes. They are pulling you home."

A sound like breaking tree branches was coming from the masts. We were afraid something was going to give way. But Mr. Brown just looked at us and smiled. "She is only talking to us a little," he said. "But she is holding."

The *Alert* flew along. At night, in our bunks, we could hear the water racing by the front of the ship.

It sounded like a roaring river. The noise of the water was so loud we had a hard time sleeping. But no one cared. We were on our way home.

Day after day the wind blew as strong as ever. The two men at the wheel were red in the face and puffing. It was all they could do just to hold on. Once, the wheel got away from them. One man was knocked across the deck into the side of the ship. The other sailor could not hold the wheel by himself.

The ship started to turn. She rolled over almost on one side. The masts could not take this much. All at once, there was a loud noise. One of the top masts was beginning to break.

Mr. Brown saw what was happening. He ran to help the man at the wheel. The two of them got the ship headed right again. But the top mast had already started to break. Before we could do anything about it, the mast gave way with a bang. Pieces of wood and rope rained down on us.

We hurried up the rigging. We had to work fast, before something else gave way. We cut away what was left of the top mast. Then we tied the ropes down. At last, everything was back in place.

We had lost the top mast, but we still had more than enough sails left. The *Alert* moved along as fast as ever. In just five days, we sailed more than 1,000 miles. Cape Horn, with its cold and snow, was far behind us now.

16 Home Again

The *Alert* kept on sailing north. There was sun-shine almost every day. And the air was getting warm again. Now we had time to clean up the ship. We washed down the deck and sanded it until it looked like new. Next, we began putting up new ropes and rigging. While some of the men were doing this, others were busy painting.

After the ship was clean and bright, we started cleaning our own things. We brought our bedding up on deck to air out. Then we washed all our clothes. When they were clean, we laid them out to dry. The warm sunshine made them smell fresh and good. Next, it was our turn. Because of the snow and cold, we had not washed for five weeks. How good that water felt! I washed myself until I just about rubbed my skin off. When we were finished, we all felt like new men.

We worked on the ship every day from morning until night. Captain Thompson wanted the *Alert* to look her best when she got to Boston. One day, I was working high up on the mast. I was standing on one of the sail yards. The yard was held in place by only one rope. But it seemed strong enough. All after-noon, I worked. When I was finished, I got ready to come down. Just as I was stepping off the yard, the rope parted. The yard fell to the deck. Had I not moved when I did, I would have been killed.

Some of the other men saw what happened. But they only laughed about it when I came down. A sailor knows that he may be killed at any time. But there is no use in thinking about it. So even when he has a very close call, he makes a joke of it. "A miss is as good as a mile," he says.

The *Alert* had a good wind in her sails. She was moving along as fast as she could. But we still had a long way to go. Days turned into weeks. We had come around Cape Horn in July. Now it was already August.

On August 7, we spotted another ship. She was the first ship we had seen for almost 100 days. It was good to see another ship after so long a time. Now we did not feel quite so alone.

The next day, we saw still another ship. Two ships in two days! This made us feel even better. And seeing the ships made us want to get home all the more. We longed to see our families and friends again. Besides this, we knew we could not last many more days without some fresh food. We had to get to Boston soon.

We had not had any fresh food for a long time. Day in and day out, we ate only salt meat and hard bread. Because of this, some of the men were getting sick. Ben, who almost had to take my place on the *Pilgrim*, was very sick.

He could do no work at all. His legs were not strong enough to hold him. His skin had turned cold and soft. And he hurt all over. We had to get some fresh food. If we did not, Ben would not live.

Three more weeks went by, then four. Each day looked like Ben's last. Now he could not even open his mouth to eat. And some of the other men were almost as sick.

Then, on September 11, the look-out spotted another ship. "Sail coming up!" he called.

In a few minutes, we all saw the ship. She was coming right at us. Soon, she was close enough for Captain Thompson to call out.

"Hello! What ship are you?" he called.

"The *Solon*, from New York," came an answering voice. "And who are you?"

"The *Alert*, around Cape Horn from California, 120 days out," said Captain Thompson. "Do you have any fresh food you can let us have?"

"Yes. We have more than enough."

Four of our sailors jumped into a boat and rowed over to the other ship. When they came back, the boat was filled with apples and cabbages. Captain Thompson called out his thanks. Then the two ships parted, each going her own way.

We had never seen anything that looked as good as those apples. Every man filled his pockets with them. We ate them one after another. The cook began making cabbage soup. But we were too hungry to wait for it. We ate the cabbages just as they were.

When the soup was done, the cook brought Ben a bowl of it. Ben could open his mouth only a little. The cook helped him drink the soup. He also brought soup to the other men who were sick.

The fresh food was just what we needed. After a few days, we all felt much better. Even Ben, who had been more sick than anyone, was getting well fast. In a week, he was back on his feet. Soon he was strong enough to work again.

On we sailed. We were not far from Boston now. But we still could not see land. Mr. Brown began to make soundings. He threw a long line over the side.

When the line hit bottom, he knew how deep the water was. We helped him pull the line back up. There was black mud on the end of it.

Mr. Brown had sailed in these waters for years. He knew them well. He could tell where we were by the color of the mud on the line. He did not even need to see the land. Captain Thompson could do the same. Mr. Brown showed the line to the captain.

"Black mud, Captain," he said. "We must be close to Block Island."

"Good," answered the captain. "Now we can head east. If the wind keeps up, we should be off Nantucket tomorrow."

"I'll take another sounding then," said Mr. Brown. "If there is dark sand on the line, we will be off Nantucket."

Early the next morning, Mr. Brown threw the line over the side. Sure enough, when we brought the line up, there was dark sand on it.

"We are almost home, my boys," said Mr. Brown. "I'll take three more soundings this morning, and three this afternoon. Watch, and you will see the color of the sand turn from dark to light. When the sand on the line is white, we will be in Boston Bay. From there, it is not far to Boston harbor."

But that afternoon, the wind stopped blowing. The air was still and quiet. The *Alert* was not moving at all. We could do nothing but wait. The sun went down and night came. Still there was no wind.

91

At last, late that night, a few puffs of wind came up. We started moving again. After a while, Mr. Brown took another sounding. The sand on the end of the line was white. We were in Boston Bay!

When my watch was over, I went below with the other men. It was quite late. But no one felt like sleeping. We sat around and talked for most of the night.

As soon as it was light, we went up on deck. Near the ship, we saw a small fishing boat heading out to sea. Then, as the sun came up, we could make out the hills of Cape Cod. Everything looked green and beautiful.

There was still not much wind. The *Alert* was not moving very fast. We could not see the harbor until late afternoon. "Hurry up, old girl," Mr. Brown said to the ship. "You only have a few miles to go."

At last, just before dark, we were in the harbor. There were boats and ships of all kinds around us. And on the land, there were houses and buildings as far as we could see. Boston seemed bigger than ever.

"Down all sails!" said Captain Thompson. "Let out the anchor!" The anchor went over the side and splashed into the water. The last time we heard that sound had been in San Diego. It was dark now, and I could see the lights of the city shining across the water. Just then, the bells in the Old South Church began to ring.

After two years before the mast, I was home.